The Ideal Customer Experience Journey

HOW TO MAKE IT A REALITY EVERY TIME

Alberto Rocha

The Ideal Customer Experience Journey / eBusiness Marketing Group. —1st ed. ISBN 978-1515115557

Contents

"You've got to start with the customer experience and work back towards the technology -not the other way around."

Steve Jobs, Co-founder and former CEO of Apple

CHAPTER 1

Introduction

How do you offer truly excellent customer service that turns each buyer into a loyal, lifelong advocate and fan? You do it through maximizing the entire customer experience. This doesn't mean simply customer service, although obviously customer service is part of it; rather, it means the overall experience your customer has with your business, which starts with their first hearing its name.

Businesses must consider the customer experience through the eyes of their customers and manage this experience to make sure it's as valuable as possible for the customer. In this course, you'll learn how to do this. By the end of the course you'll have a detailed understanding of the customer experience you offer and legitimate ways you can improve and streamline it.

In this course, you will:

- Define what the customer experience is and why it's so important.

- Map the customer experience that you currently offer your customers.

- Analyze your map to identify weak areas that need improvement or areas where there are potential problems.

- Describe the elements that make a good customer experience, as well as examples of these elements in real life.

- Go through the map you created and at each point make improvements that will impact the experience as a whole

- Walk away from the course with goals, specific tasks, and deadlines for getting the improvements done.

The customer experience has gained a great deal of attention in the business world in recent years, with many businesses seeing firsthand the tremendous difference it makes when they take control of the experience and maximize it. Understanding and maximizing the customer experience is what separates decent companies from those that build strong, loyal relationships with their customers.

CHAPTER 2

What is the 'Customer Experience'

L et's start by defining exactly what we mean by the customer experience, also known as CX. To get a good grasp on this somewhat difficult concept, let's look at a few different definitions for comparison. There are many definitions given below, but we'll summarize at the end with a simple, clear definition useful for this course.

The company *Beyond Philosophy*, which leads organizations to create good customer experiences, defines it as, "an interaction between an organization and a customer as perceived through a customer's conscious and subconscious mind. It is a blend of an organization's rational performance, the senses stimulated and the emotions evoked and intuitively measured against customer expectations across all moments of contact."

Avaya, another company that specializes in this field, calls it, "the discipline of managing and treating customer relationships as assets with the goal of transforming satisfied customers into loyal customers, and loyal customers into advocates of your brand."

An article on the **Harvard Business Review** defines it as the journey the customer takes with your company from the very first time they become aware of it until the very end. The HBR definition emphasizes that it is more than just the many touch points a customer has with you or the life of just one sale.

BusinessDictionary.com defines it as, "The entirety of the interactions a customer has with a company and its products. Understanding the customer experience is an integral part of customer relationship management. The overall experience reflects how the customer feels about the company and its offerings. Surveys, feedback forms and other data collection techniques help a company to determine the customer experience."

Finally, we can look at **Wikipedia's definition**: "Customer experience (CX) is the product of an interaction between an organization and a customer over the duration of their relationship. This interaction includes a customer's attraction, awareness, discovery, cultivation, advocacy and purchase and use of a service. It is measured by the individual's experience during all points of contact against the individual's expectations."

So, what can we deduce from all of these definitions? To summarize:

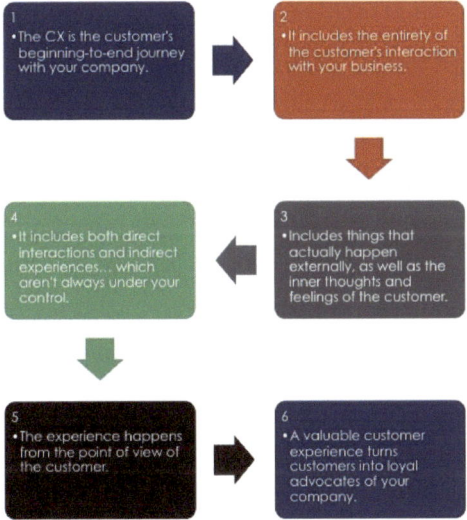

- The CX is more than just a routine interaction or one sale, but the customer's beginning-to-end journey with your company.

- It includes the entirety of the customer's interaction with your business.

- It includes things that actually happen externally, as well as the inner thoughts and feelings of the customer.

- It includes both direct interactions and indirect experiences, such as when a customer hears about your brand which aren't always under your control.

- The experience happens from the point of view of the customer.

- Good interactions with your customer help them buy from you, but a valuable customer experience turns customers into loyal advocates of your company.

Why Customer Experience Is So Important

"Customers remember experiences, not your brand logo."

Martin Zwilling

The customer experience is important because every aspect of your relationship and interactions with the customer spring from it. It's the "big picture" view of this complicated relationship. To drive home just how important it is, here are some things to consider:

- A study by **Strativity Group** in 2009 found that 860 corporate executives who increased their investment in understanding and managing their customer experience saw higher customer referral rates and rates of customer satisfaction.

- According to Beyond Philosophy, a good customer experience makes acquiring customers easier, drives customer loyalty and helps companies effortlessly improve their customer retention.

- A good customer experience applies the "wow factor", which means that it exceeds customer expectations. This is a proven way to keep customers coming back for more.

- It also keeps your customers from going to one of your competitors to get their needs met. People like to buy from places that make them feel good. Since the customer experience is closely associated with the customer's feelings and psychology, it's effective at retaining customers.

- With a good customer experience, you don't have to try so hard to develop an advantage over your competitors. You don't have to lower your price because customers will gladly pay more for a good customer experience.

- If you offer an outstanding customer experience, this helps to differentiate you from other companies. It's very powerful in branding your company. You can use this point of differentiation to your advantage.

- The investment you make in customer experience research will pay off in real results. Analytics and sales data can help a great deal in developing your strategies, but there's nothing as effective as direct feedback from your customers themselves.

Finally, a nice thing to know about customer experience is that few companies invest in it, which means that if your company does so, you'll have a great advantage over others. A report by *Econsultancy* found that only about 20% of companies have a well-developed customer experience strategy. This means it's a huge opportunity for those that choose to invest.

The Damage a Bad Customer Experience Can Do

A good customer experience works because of the "wow" factor, where customer expectations are exceeded. A bad customer experience results from the opposite, where the experience falls short of the customer's expectations.

When companies cut costs in the area of customer experience, they really endanger their long-term relationships with customers. This is because the long-term relationship can be severely damaged by one bad purchasing experience, one negative thing heard about the company indirectly, or any other small bump in the road. This threatens long-term revenue and it means you have to work harder to acquire customers to make up for those you lose.

A bad customer experience also tends to spiral out of control and lead to an even worse reputation among customers. This is because of word-of-mouth. When a customer has a bad experience with your company, they're likely to tell others. With social media and review sites today, this is especially damaging, and this is an area where you have no control.

The Key Stages of the Customer Experience

Now that we've defined the customer experience and underlined the importance of it, let's take a closer look at the key stages where customers have experiences with your business. Not all of these stages apply to all businesses, but they're fairly universal.

Brand Awareness. This is where a customer first learns about your brand. It's where you come across their radar for the first time. This could be through ads, online content, the recommendation of a friend, seeing your storefront, etc.

Interest. The next stage is where the customer begins to take an interest in your products or services. They move from simple awareness of your brand to actively seeking out more information. They may research your company, look at your website, or ask the friend that recommended you about you.

A Taste of Your Offering. At this stage, the customer gets their first real taste of what you have to offer. This could be through a free trial, a freebie, free online content, or a situation where they meet a representative of your company for a sample.

Purchase. This is the stage where the customer makes their first purchase of your product or service. This is not just the moment of actually buying the product, but includes every stage of the purchase process along the way.

Use of Product or Service. After purchasing the product or service, your customer will use it, which is a major part of the customer experience. This is where their expectations are fulfilled, disappointed or wowed. This stage includes the quality of the product, its delivery and implementation, and so on.

Post-Purchase. This stage includes all that happens after the initial purchase. At this stage, you may be contacting the customer to provide more content, information or deals, or to request feedback or comments from them.

Repeat Purchases. This is really part of the post-purchase stage, but it's important to focus specifically on each additional purchase in the same way as the first one. Also, this stage includes cross-sells, upsells, down-sells, customer loyalty deals, and so on.

Referral Process. Your company's referral process is an important stage. This is where the customer tells others about you, shares content about you on social media, and so on. It includes things like your communications regarding referrals such as thank-you emails.

Customer Service. At any point where you have customer service processes, you'll need to consider the customer experience carefully. This is not really a stage by itself, but is a thread that runs through various stages from beginning to end.

Another way to think about customer experience is by breaking it down into four categories of experiences:

Discovery Experiences:	Relationship Experiences:	Purchase Experiences:	Follow-Up Experiences:
• Experiences that involve customers seeking information about you that include visibility, online content, awareness, and so on.	• Includes everything you do to build a relationship with both your prospects and customers.	• Includes trying out your products, purchasing your products, implementing them and dealing with problems with them.	• Everything involved in continuing your relationship after the purchase including further sales and referrals.

- *Discovery Experiences*: These are experiences that involve customers seeking information about you that include visibility, online content, awareness, and so on.

- *Relationship Experiences*: This category includes everything you do to build a relationship with both your prospects and customers.

- *Purchase Experiences*: This includes trying out your products, purchasing your products, implementing them and dealing with problems with them.

- *Follow-Up Experiences*: These experiences include everything involved in continuing your relationship after the purchase including further sales and referrals.

If this sounds a bit complicated now, don't worry. You're not supposed to understand it yet. We're taking a big picture view and in the next few modules, we'll get more specific.

What you'll do in the next module is map out the customer experience you currently have with your customers. You'll create a "Customer Experience Map" that includes absolutely everything. In the process, you'll define what's ideal for your business – things like your value proposition, customer persona, branding, corporate culture, etc. – and then identify what areas most impact your customer experience. You'll determine what's needed and where there are potential breakdown points that you need to be careful of.

Learning Activity

1. Identify a product or service you've purchased several times, preferable one you've recommended to others. For example, it could be a restaurant you go to regularly, a store you love to shop at, a dentist who's taken good care of you, a business service you rely on every month, etc.

2. Think about what makes you feel so good about your experience with this company.

    i.   How did you first hear about it?

    ii.   Why did you decide to use/buy it?

    iii.   What do you love most?

    iv.   Why do you or would you recommend it to your friends?.

CHAPTER 3

Map Your Current Customer Experience

In this module, we're going to look at your business and where it currently stands in terms of the customer experience. We'll identify where the touch points are that affect the customer experience, both directly and indirectly. By the end of the module, you'll have a big-picture view so that you can then identify key specific areas for making improvements.

The map you'll make now is a visual representation of the story of your company through the eyes of your customer. It will tell the story of their entire relationship over time and across communication channels. You can't represent everything visually. You'll need to write some text to fill in details. But the map will give you the necessary big-picture view.

In order to get this big-picture view, you may want to use some type of tool for mapping. A worksheet is provided. You can also use a mind map, either through a mind mapping program or with a simple pencil and paper, or a spreadsheet if you're more comfortable with that.

In this module, you'll brainstorm and draw your map. You'll see some samples and get some ideas for brainstorming that will help you create that map.

Here are the steps to take in order to create your map:

Create a Persona

Every story needs a main character. The main character of this story is your customer. You should already have a target customer profile created for your business. This is the ideal customer who wants or needs your products and to whom you can offer the most possible value. At the starting point of your map, define this person and provide data about them. This persona should include your customer's goals, needs and desires. You'll also need to identify each goal at each stage or touch point during the process, which we'll talk about in a second.

Stages of the Customer Experience

Next, identify the stages your customer goes through as they go on their journey. Look at the stages from the last module and modify as necessary. Put yourself in the shoes of your customer and imagine what stages they go through with your company.

Touch Points with Your Customer

Identify every touch point you have with your customer. It's important to have good customer interactions at every touch point. Likewise, at any given touch point, a bad experience or an experience that falls short of expectations, could be disastrous to the whole. To make your map, you need to go through each of the touch points below and examine the process through the eyes of your customer.

Your Website. A company's website is a common touch point, especially at the beginning (the awareness stage). Your site is where a prospect will learn more about your business before deciding whether or not to buy from you.

Advertising. Your ads, whether in print or online, are another key touch point for the beginning of your relationship with the customer.

Online Content. Online content will be a touch point in the initial stages as well as throughout, especially if content marketing is a regular part of spreading awareness and building a relationship with your customer.

Networking and Referrals. If someone refers you to a potential customer, this is a touch point. Any contact you have with customers through networking is also a touch point. This includes networking events as well as informal networking and online networking.

Events and Conventions. A good touch point that affects customer experience is offline events and conventions. If your business participates in any type of offline event, this is a key venue for interaction with your customers.

Physical Store. If you have a brick-and-mortar store, this is an important touch point, even if you do much of your business online. Some of the most affecting experiences your customers will have with your brand will be here, in the flesh.

Your Value Proposition. Your value proposition communicates what you offer and sets expectations with your customers. Therefore, it's a key touch point.

Social Media. Social media is a touch point for everything from initial awareness to maintaining relationships with customers.

Design. The design language you use has an influence on customer experience.

Your Employees. Every member of your staff that has contact with customers plays a part. In addition to customer service, they also spread your company's culture. Your organization's people are an integral part of your map.

SEO. SEO has an impact on customer experience on a number of ways. For one, it's important for awareness. But it can also damage trust if your website doesn't show up for the searches your customers expect it to show up for.

Social Proof. The social proof you offer, whether as testimonials, references or in whatever form, is important in setting customer expectations. When one person received certain results from your product or service, others expect to receive these results as well.

Reputation. Third-party reviews, mentions in blogs, and social media comments all play a part in establishing your reputation. A good or bad reputation contributes as an indirect aspect of the customer experience.

PR. PR includes third-party mentions in official media like TV or articles. These aren't paid advertisements or customer reviews, but write-ups or stories in mass media.

Sales Process. Each step of the sales process offers a touch point. These touch points are important for showing your commitment to customer service and your consistency.

Trial Offers and Freebies. Each sample, trial or freebie you offer is a touch point. This includes things like free content you give away as an enticement for website visitors to sign up for your email list.

Follow-ups. Whenever you follow-up with your customer, whether to say thank you or to make another offer, you have an important touch point.

Delivery. If any aspect of your service requires deliver, this is an important area in terms of customer satisfaction.

Customer Support. After-purchase support to help customers use or implement your products, including refunds, returns or any other special support you offer, offers very important touch points.

Incentive and Loyalty Programs. If you offer incentive or loyalty programs to your customers, this is one way they get to experience your service.

Communications. All communications with your customers from the very beginning of the awareness stage to the ongoing purchase stage are very important touch points.

Communication Channels

The next important consideration is to identify communication channels. These are the ways that you communicate with your customers. They should be as specific as possible. Don't use terms like "the internet," "advertising" or "social media." Identify specific sites, blogs, online forums, advertising media, social media sites, and so on.

Think of channels as venues where touch points take place. For example, your offline store is a channel as well as a touch point. It's a place where interaction between you and your customers happens.

Timeline

Wherever possible, add a specific timeframe to the stages or interactions on your map. Areas that are time sensitive include deliver times, follow-ups, communications with your customer, and so on. You can also add times wherever you have specific data, such as how long it takes from the initial contact with your company to first purchase. Timeframe is a major factor in customer experience, and if there are areas where your services take too long, this will be an area to improve.

Emotional Moments or Moments of Truth

Try to pinpoint specific moments during each process where your customers experience emotions or moments of truth. These might be things like the feeling of satisfaction after first using your product or the moment when the customer realizes that your offering is unique. If there are certain important moments in the customer's story that you know of, add them here.

Supporting Cast

You already identified the main character – your customer. You should also add anyone else that plays a part in the customer experience. This includes anyone from your company that has direct contact with your customer, as well as other people such as friends who tell the customer about your company.

Drawing Your Customer Experience Map

Once you have all of your touch points identified, it's time to create your customer experience map. This is a map that starts at the earliest stages of your customer's awareness and leads eventually to their loyal patronage of your business.

Let's take a look at a few examples from some companies who have spent a lot of time at the customer experience mapping process.

You won't necessarily be creating maps as complex as these, but they'll give you an idea of what's possible.

Take note of how they identify touchpoints and emotion.

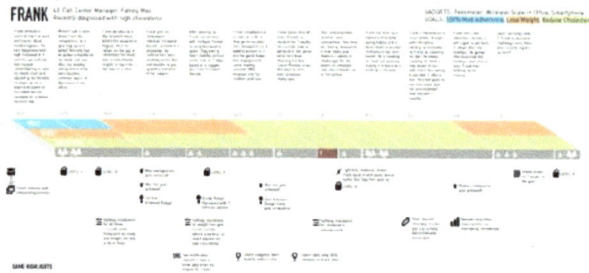

Mad Pow's Player Journey. Courtesy of UX Mastery.

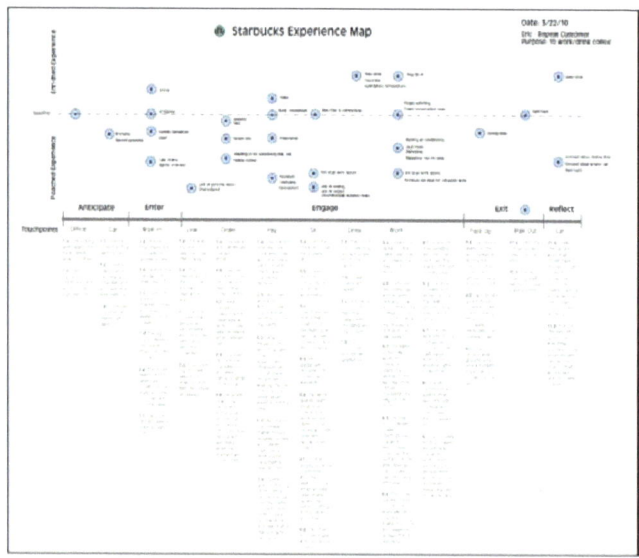

Starbucks Experience Map. Courtesy of UX-Lady.com

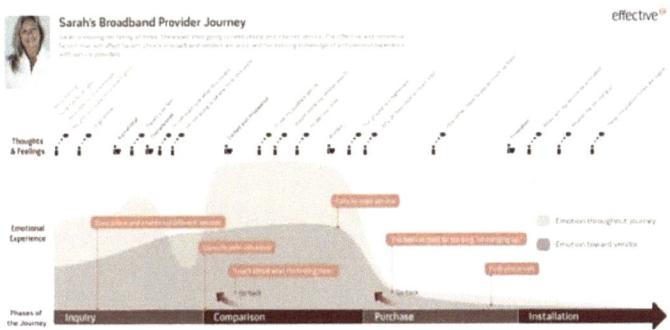

Sarah's Broadband Provider Map. Courtesy of UXMatters

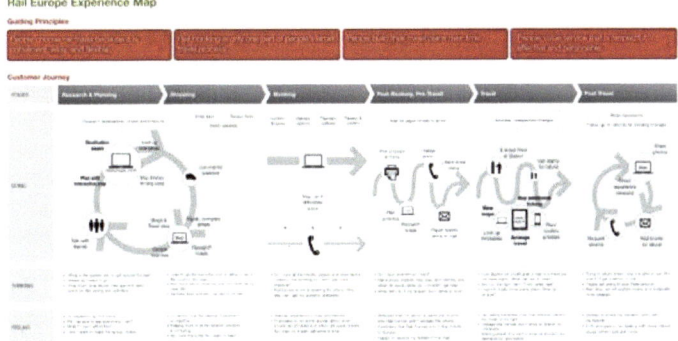

Rail Europe Experience Map. Courtesy of Coprosystem.co.jp

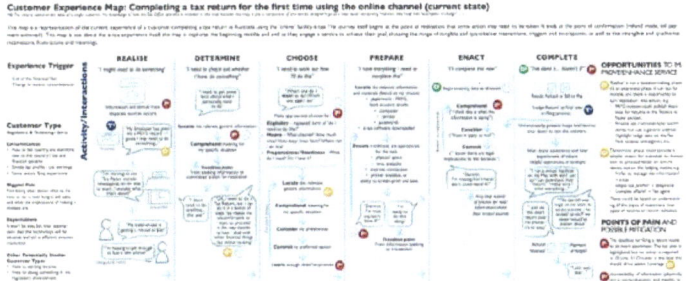

Completing a Tax Return Online for the First Time. Courtesy of Desonance

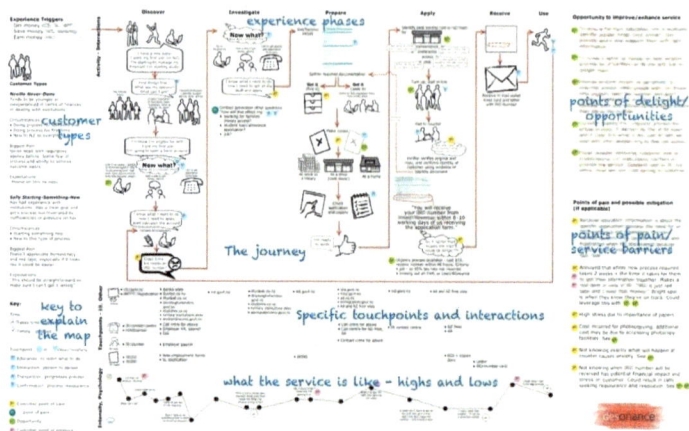

Template courtesy of Desonance

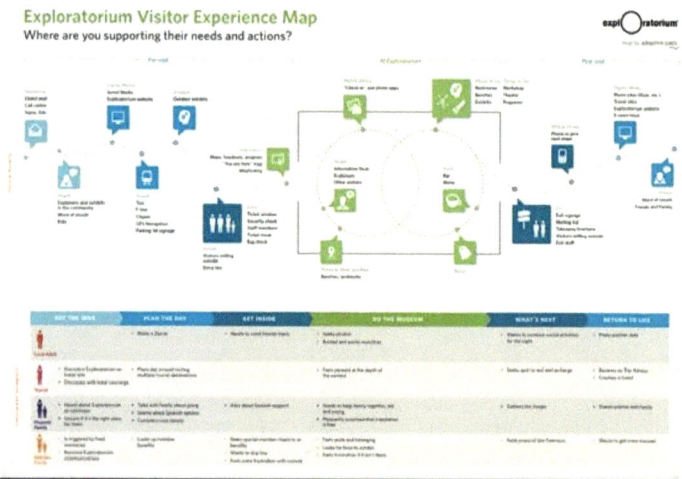

Exploratorium Visitor Experience Map 1. Courtesy of Adaptive Path

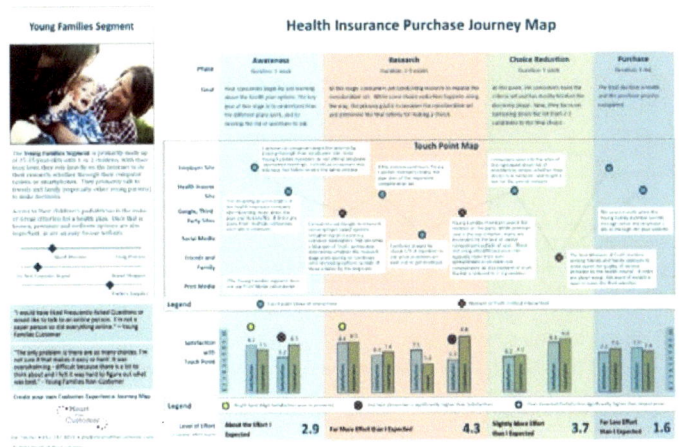

Health Insurance Purchase Journey Map. Courtesy of
HeartOfTheCustomer.Com

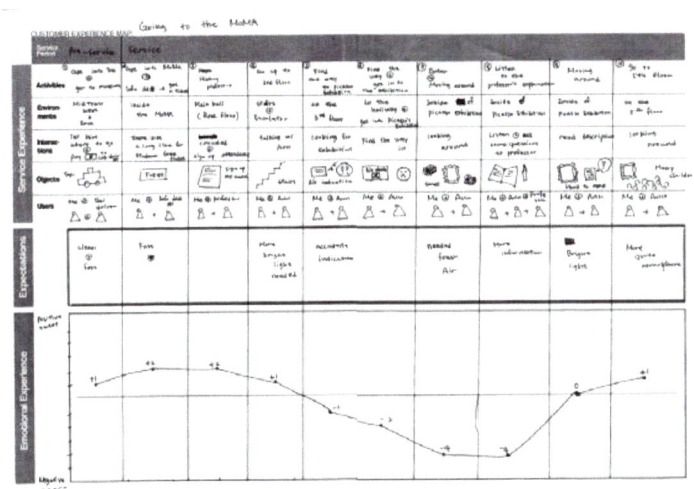

Going to the MOMA. Courtesy of SueDesign

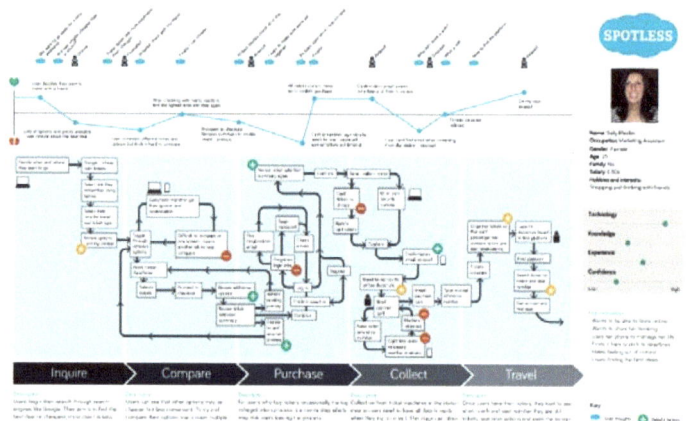

Example from Spotless

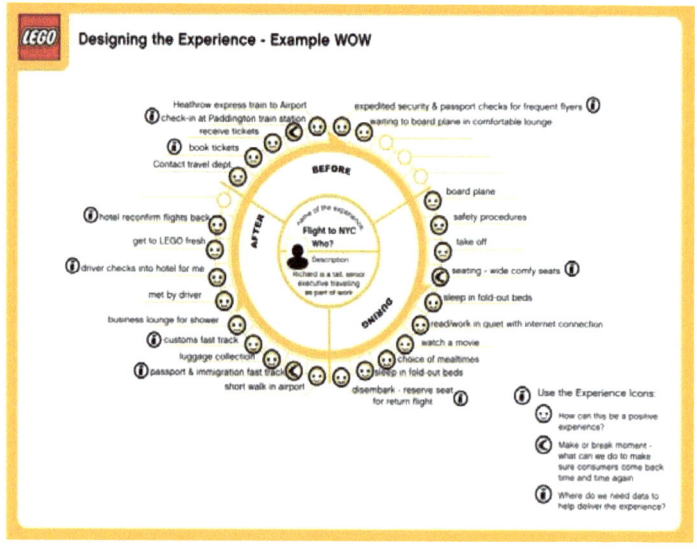

Lego Experience. Courtesy of Lego

Learning Activity:

1. Use the provided worksheet or your own tool, such as a mind map, white board, or Gantt chart, to map out as much of your own business's customer experience as you can.

   If you want, you can use just the first part of the worksheet with the simpler map of the 4 types of experiences, especially if your business doesn't follow a linear process

2. If possible, ask one of your long-term, loyal customers to assess the map you've created and see if you missed anything.

CHAPTER 4

The Key Elements of an Ideal Customer Experience

I n this module, we're going to look at the key elements that create a good customer experience. You can check these against the map that you've made to make sure they're in alignment. If they're not, you'll know exactly which areas need to be addressed when you re-do your map and make the necessary changes to the customer experience your business offers.

The Ideal Customer Experience Is a Core Part of a Brand

Consistency is the key to branding. Your customer experience should be consistent from beginning to end. Achieving this consistency starts with clearly defining your brand. If you haven't already done this, do it now. Make sure that you effectively communicate this brand to your target market. Then, make sure that every touch point, interaction and other part of the customer experience is consistent with that.

Identify Your Core Values

Your core values should be well identified. These values include how you want people to feel, what type of relationship you want to have with your customers, and what you want them to say about you. All of this drives what you do to create the ideal experience.

Your value proposition is also key in establishing customer expectations and the key to creating a good customer experience is defining and meeting those expectations. Remember that even if your core values are accurate, you still need to communicate them effectively to your customers.

The Customer Experience Is a Relationship

Since the customer experience is the relationship between your company and your customer, you need to identify what kind of relationship this would be. Some things to ask yourself here include:

- The image you want to have in your customers' minds.

- The emotions you want interactions with your company to spark in customers.

- The culture of your company that you want to convey to your customers.

- Your company's personality and how your customers see it.

Remember how we made a customer persona in the last module? Knowing your customer is essential to creating a good customer experience. You need a deep understanding of your customer. Amazon CEO Jeff Bezos famously has an empty chair at company meetings, which he says is reserved for the customer. He says the empty chair is the most important person in the room.

This is how you should go about designing your customer experience. Know their needs and goals. Understand their motivations. Gain an understanding of why they behave in certain ways. Use real customer data to glean these insights.

The more you personalize the experience and make it feel like a relationship, the more easily you can create an ideal customer experience.

Indirect Branding and the Customer Experience

When we consider branding, we tend to think in big brush strokes. But there are many small factors that also contribute to the brand image in the minds of your customers. Branding factors that indirectly affect the customer relationship include graphics, company culture, the appearance or attire of your employees, and so on. Consider these factors as well

Specific Things That Make Your Business Unique

The unique things you do that are specific to your company set it apart from others. This is why these elements are very important in the overall customer experience. It's most likely that these are the things that your customers value about you most. These are the reasons they don't go to a competitor. Ask yourself: What's specific about how you do business?

You should summarize this as your Unique Value Proposition. This is a statement that clearly and concisely communicates to the customer exactly what it is that makes your company unique. It tells them what you do and how you do it in a way that's different from all of your competitors. In other words, it's the unique reason why a person buys from you. It's your promise to your customer.

The best way to discover this uniqueness is to ask your customers directly. Seek feedback and let them tell you, rather than trying to come up with your company's unique points on your own.

The Customer Experience Is Emotional

The customer experience focuses not only on the nuts and bolts of the interactions you have with your customer. You also need to consider the customer's emotions. You identified emotional moments in the last module and you should have a deep understanding of how your customer thinks and feels.

A well-designed customer experience triggers emotions in customers that positively affect them, leading to customer retention and loyalty. A good customer experience transcends the rational or physical attributes of your product or service.

A Great Customer Experience Exceeds Expectations

A really great customer experience stirs emotions, builds a bond and inspires loyalty through what we call "the wow factor," or in other words, by exceeding the customer's expectations (make them say "wow").

Things that create this experience don't have to be monumental and earth shattering. They could be extremely small and simple things such as:

- *A restaurant* that provides nice baskets where you can store bags and accessories.

- *A business* that doesn't have an automated phone system but actually answers the telephone when you call with a real human representative of the company.

- *A retail store* that gives you handy wipes or offers disinfectant spray at the door.

- *A retail business* that ensures its employees are always friendly and smiling.

- *A hotel* that offers complementary newspapers, bathrobes or other items.

- *A car wash* or other service where the manager takes a shift washing windows and chatting with customers.

There are several ways you can supply the wow factor. One is to simply find ways to delight the customer. Another is to anticipate their wants and desires, and deliver them before they ask. Like the car wash manager example, you can deliver the wow factor by personalizing your service in some way. It also involves an attention to the little details.

The wow factor works to get people talking about your business.

To better illustrate the elements we've discussed in this module, let's look at some examples of companies that have managed to create stellar customer experiences.

Oscar

Oscar is a health insurance provider that serves New York only. What makes Oscar unique among healthcare providers is that they "speak human." Health insurance is notoriously hard to understand, so it's Oscar's mission and brand to make it simple. Starting with its simple Google-like website, it offers easy-to-understand explanations of its plans in language any layperson can easily understand.

To help customers choose the right plan, it asks a few simple questions. Customers can enter in a simple phrase like, "I am married with two kids. I make $40,000 per year. My zip code is 10012." The website will then return results that match what the customer has entered.

Everything Oscar offers is this user-friendly and layperson-oriented, so from beginning to end, it creates a consistent customer experience that makes it easy to select the right health insurance policy.

Zipcar

Zipcar is a company that offers car sharing as an alternative to car rental. It offers an excellent customer experience from beginning to end for one simple reason – it knows its customers so well. Zipcar users are mobile people who need to get where they need to go with as little fuss as possible.

Zipcar tailors its customer experience to its customers in a number of ways. One way that it does this is by offering the rules and terms upfront and in a very easy-to-understand way (its customers don't have time to dig through fine print). Car rental companies are notorious for having confusing terms.

Amazon

Amazon has made itself the world's biggest online retailer by making everything it does completely customer-centric. CEO Jeff Bezos has always stated this as the aim of the company. Every aspect of the experience of shopping with Amazon is centered around the customer. Peer-to-peer reviews and customer communities put customers in charge and give them a place to share their interests with one another. This, along with its excellent terms of service, has helped turn it into the ecommerce giant it is today. At no point in your experience with Amazon do you feel like it's not about you, the customer.

Apple

Apple has created a kind of cult of loyal customers around its followers. We all know someone who talks endlessly about the virtues of Apple. When you discover a new feature or gadget, you rush online to tell everyone about it. When you have trouble using one of the company's products, you get on a forum and someone is there to tell you how to fix it. Apple has a community and it can leverage its connectedness.

Publix

Publix is like a version of Wal-Mart that not only treats its workers well but strives to empower them. Nearly all workers are also owners. The result is a company that's exceedingly people-oriented and it shows in how it treats its customers.

There's a well-known story of a Publix employee named Gage Boucher in Florida who tied an elderly shopper's shoe for him because he was unable to. Another shopper took a picture and posted it online, where it quickly went viral and earned the company a great deal of attention. Seeing the picture, which was candidly shot during the course of any old business day, it's easy to imagine that acts of kindness like this are common everyday occurrences.

IKEA

IKEA is a company that knows its customers well. It also realizes that buying home furnishings is about more than just functionality and cost. It's also about expressing yourself, or in effect, creating a "brand" for your home. IKEA specializes in offering home furnishings that help its customers accomplish this.

One way it does this is by creating a community of IKEA fans, who share with each other their projects and ask each other for ideas. Through online communities, they can discuss their artist home decorating ideas and get feedback from other like-minded customers.

Learning Activity:

Before going back to your customer experience map, think about the following:

1. What are the top 3 core values of your business?

2. What emotions do you want your customers to feel about your business?

3. What type of relationship do you want to have with customers? (For example, how personal vs professional)

4. What do you want your customers to say about their experience with your business?

CHAPTER 5

Map Your Business's Ideal Customer Experience

Now that you've learned the elements that make a great customer experience, it's time to go back to your present customer experience map and start identifying how it should look. With your target customer in mind, you'll identify what you need to change, what you need to add, and what you need to do differently.

The Big Picture

Start by looking at each key stage of the customer experience. Go through the stages outlined in the first module: awareness, lead generation, relationship-building, becoming a customer, follow-up, and whichever other stages you chose to focus on.

At each stage, choose a few things to change, add or do differently. How many you should consider depends on the complexity of your business. Try to choose only three to five things at each stage for now. You may think of more things later during this process.

Once you've covered these areas generally and thought of a few things you can do to maximize the customer experience, go through your map in more detail. At each touch point and every other stage of your map, see what you can change.

While considering changes to be made, keep central in your mind:

- Your customer persona/ target market.
- Your business's brand, Unique Value Proposition and core values.

Areas to Consider

You should take stock of not only where customers interact with your business, but every aspect of it. Remember how Zappos' five-week training had a major impact on customer service, or Publix's largely employee-owned structure led to a customer-centered experience? These are areas of a business that are "behind the scenes." The customer experience includes every aspect, even those aspects where there is no direct contact with customers.

Areas to consider include:

Content

The content you share with your customers needs to be in keeping with the overall experience they have with your brand. It should be "on brand" and indirectly convey what your company is all about.

You should consider every single piece of content that you publish. This includes things like website content, blog posts, articles, social media posts, videos, informational pamphlets, infographics, podcasts and teleseminars. Every one of these types of content contributes to the customer experience.

Guidelines/Standards

Your company's internal rules and standards should be created with the customer experience in mind. Consider how each policy could possibly affect the experience. Guidelines and standards range from small details like the fonts or images you use in documents to larger and more important things like quality standards for your products.

Processes/Systems

The protocols and operating procedures of your company can have a major impact on the customer experience so they also need to be established with this in mind.

Even business processes that don't deal with customers directly can have an impact. Areas like accounting, IT policies, protocols for meetings, routine web traffic analyses and so on can all have an impact on company culture, which can be felt in some ways by customers indirectly.

Training

The training you offer your employees, especially which relates to customer service, is very important in creating the customer experience. It also creates your company's culture, which has a direct effect.

Lack of training can lead to poor morale among workers which leads to bad customer service. Each employee needs to have the proper training in order to deal with customers confidently and professionally. It's also essential that through training, your employees understand thoroughly your products and services so that they can provide the information customers need about them.

Communication

How you communicate both within your company and with the public outside has a major influence on your customers. Internal communications are important for establishing your company culture and also ensuring productivity. For example, if you can communicate quickly with a different department in order to answer a customer's question, you can provide quicker service to the customer.

Things to consider about customer communication include communication style (how aggressive or passive), communication channels, the extent to which communications are promotional, specific communication protocols (or scripts) all should be considered.

People

Many people involved with your business in various capacities have an influence. This includes employees (both those on the "front lines" and those behind the scenes), business associates, sponsors, brand advocates, and so on.

For example, you may outsource your product manufacturing to a third party company. This company's quality standards and business processes have a direct impact on the product's quality, which directly impacts the customer's experience of the product. If you have an affiliate program, everything your affiliates do has a direct impact on your reputation and how the public see your company. You have to consider absolutely everyone associated with your brand.

Mapping your customer experience can be a long and involved process, depending on how detailed a map you're making. You don't have to try to do it all at once. You also don't have to do it all by yourself. Enlist employees, colleagues or others whose input you value.

Learning Activity:

1. Using the worksheet provided, or your own visual tool, start mapping the ideal experience you want your customers to have. Review the work you did in the previous module and keep that in mind as you complete your new map.

2. For each stage of the experience, identify actions you'll take to make that ideal experience you just described a reality. Include things like

    i. Content you can create

    ii. Guidelines or standards you can define

    iii. Processes or systems you can implement

    iv. Training you can conduct

    v. Communication methods or protocols

    vi. People to hire or align with

CHAPTER 6

Identify and Prevent Potential Breakdown Points

I n this module, we'll identify some areas and trouble spots you're likely to have in your map. By learning these ahead of time, you can figure out ways to prevent the customer experience from breaking down.

Response Time

Regardless of your type of business or brand, response time to inquiries and support requests must be fast. One of the easiest ways to lose trust is to respond slowly to customers. This is a major reason that customers leave one company and turn to another. It's also a good way to apply the wow factor, as many companies don't reply promptly.

Customer Support Replies

The friendliness and level of professionalism of your customer support replies are also extremely important. It's essential that your phone support staff do everything in their power to make sure the customer is happy.

For example, suppose that a customer has a complaint about a product they purchased from your company. If they can't get a hold of anyone in a timely manner, this is potentially damaging. If the representative they speak to is rude or if they feel that they are rude, this could cause further problems. Even if communication is civil, miscommunications can cause a breakdown.

If your representative is troubleshooting a technical problem with a customer and they can't express clearly what they need the customer to do, this can make the entire process much more complicated than it needs to be. Your commitment to ease-of-use for the customer could be tarnished by these communication problems.

Direct Communications

In addition to telephone communications, pay close attention to any kind of direct communication, such as emails, face-to-face meetings, and so on. Your employees must be well-trained when it comes to talking to customers. Any slip-up here could serious damage the experience for the customer.

Again, communication could pose a problem. If the customer perceives your company's representative as being rude or if communication isn't clear, this could cause a break down. Things like attitude, body language and facial expression are small details that could also impact a face-to-face encounter.

Social Media Responses

Social media is very important in the customer experience today. When someone asks a question, leaves a comment or sends a message on social media, it's critical that you act quickly and appropriately. Poor social media communications, especially when public, can seriously hurt the experience of your customers.

Let's imagine that a customer is unhappy with your online chat support service and airs their grievance on Facebook in front of their hundreds of friends. This is potentially disastrous to your company's reputation, but it can be mitigated if you act quickly, and even turned into a good opportunity.

A good way to handle the situation would be to reply to the customer with an apology and a request for clarification. Ask them to explain exactly what happened. Empathize with the customer, explain any misunderstanding, and offer somehow to make it better for them. The end result is that their hundreds of friends can see that you're a company that, even though maybe not perfect, is willing to improve for its highly-valued customers.

Automated Systems

Some type of automated system is essential to any business running smoothly, especially when it starts experiencing a high volume of sales or other customer interactions. But automated systems pose a huge risk in that they may not work properly.

Always check out your automated systems by trying them out yourself as the customer (for example, go through your site's shopping cart and make a purchase). Make this a routine part of your business so that you can correct any problems before customers experience them. Make sure also to keep all automated systems updated.

For example, let's say that you're communicating with your customers through an email list. Your autoresponder automates the process of sending out messages. However, there's a mistake with the email message template you're using and it addresses your recipients as something like "name here" instead of their actual names.

This is a minor mistake and many recipients would shrug it off. But it also shows that you're a company that doesn't pay attention to detail. It could lead the customer to ask, "What else are they sloppy about? Handling my personal data maybe?"

Over-Promotion

It's often hard to walk the fine line between promoting enough and over-promoting. While not promoting enough could mean your message getting lost on your customers, over-promotion can definitely impact the customer experience negatively.

If you're using Facebook to communicate with your customers and all of your messages are promotional, this could lead your followers to tune you out. They'll skip past your updates or block them entirely. You'll look like a company that only communicates when it wants something.

On the other hand, if you send out useful and interesting content, the kind of updates your customers look forward to, you'll be regarded as a trusted source of information and entertainment, personalizing your brand and increasing the likelihood people will buy from you.

When in doubt, err on the side of less promotion. Don't promote on social media or in online forums. Try to let your content do the promoting for you, and only promote on media that is strictly promotional (your website, a marketing brochure, an advertisement, etc.). Also when in doubt, you can ask for a third-party opinion about whether your promotion is tasteful or not.

Technological Breakdowns

There are many little things that can go wrong technologically. Your website may not load well on mobiles or your phones might be down and unable to take calls. This is understandable but it can still impact the customer experience. Make all the effort necessary to ensure that the technological aspects of your business are up-to-date and running smoothly. Identify points in your map where a technological failure would be disastrous, and make changes so that it won't.

Quality Issues

The quality of your products and services must be consistent. Try to identify anything that poses a risk to this consistency. Customers come to expect this consistency and if they receive a shoddy product or bad service even once, it can impact their entire relationship with your business. A good business is one that never lets its customers down (remember expectations here).

Lack of Follow-up

After a sale, there should always be a follow-up. This is an important part of the customer experience because it solidifies the relationship you have with your customer. It also shows that you're interested in building this relationship and not just one sale. Make sure that you have some kind of follow-up in place and that it's ongoing.

Where Does Your Customer Experience Break Down?

It may not always be obvious at which points during the customer journey there are breakdowns that affect the overall experience. You may be able to identify some just from what you know about your business, but a better way is to gather objective data telling you exactly where and how it's happening.

Sources of this data include:

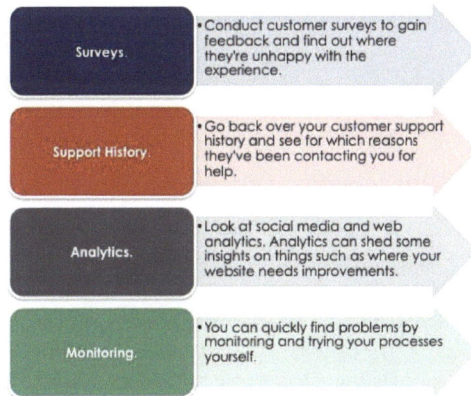

- **Surveys**. You can conduct customer surveys to gain their feedback and find out where they're unhappy with the experience. One bonus of doing this is that you engage your customers, getting them actively involved, and show that you're concerned.

- **Support History**. Go back over your customer support history and see for which reasons they've been contacting you for help. You'll quickly see which areas need changes.

- *Analytics*. Look at social media and web analytics. Analytics can shed some insights on things such as where your website needs improvements. You can tell this by seeing where customers are leaving your site.

- *Monitoring*. As mentioned above in relation to automated systems and technological aspects of your business, you can quickly find problems by monitoring and trying your processes yourself.

Best Practices for Preventing Breakdowns

Preventing these breakdowns should be a regular part of your business operations. There are several ways you can do this:

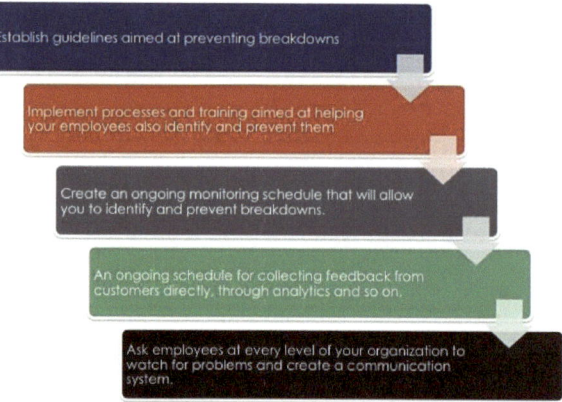

Establish guidelines aimed at preventing breakdowns

Implement processes and training aimed at helping your employees also identify and prevent them

Create an ongoing monitoring schedule that will allow you to identify and prevent breakdowns.

An ongoing schedule for collecting feedback from customers directly, through analytics and so on.

Ask employees at every level of your organization to watch for problems and create a communication system.

- Establishing guidelines aimed at preventing breakdowns

- Implementing processes and training aimed at helping your employees also identify and prevent them

- An ongoing monitoring schedule that will allow you to identify and prevent breakdowns before your customers experience them.

- An ongoing schedule for collecting feedback from customers directly, through analytics and so on.

- Ask employees at every level of your organization to watch for problems and create a communication system where they can flag and direct your attention to them (or the attention of whoever handles these concerns).

Learning Activity:

Use the provided worksheet to note places where your current customer experience is most at risk, or which already needs immediate attention.

1. *Review each key area listed* in the module for potential breakdowns. Conduct research if necessary if you're not sure of the current quality.

2. *Mark areas that need immediate attention* and what actions you need to take Note at least 3 steps you will take to prevent potential breakdowns in the customer experience

CHAPTER 7

Conclusion and Next Steps

Now that you've mapped your current customer experience and identified the ways you need to change it, you're ready to get started streamlining and implementing a better customer journey. It's time to go back over the work you've done throughout this course and figure out the next steps you need to take. For each of these action steps, set a deadline to make sure it gets done.

In this course, you've learned:

- What the customer experience is and all of the reasons that it's so important for your business.

- How to create a map of your customer experience using guidelines and provided examples.

- The elements of a good customer experience and how you can work these elements into yours.

- How to create the ideal customer experience and implement the necessary changes you've identified in your current one.

- The areas most at risk of breaking down and how you can prevent these breakdowns.

By working through the course, you've already gotten a good start on creating the right customer experience for your customers. Now, take the next steps and set deadlines for each so that you'll have a solid timeframe for getting them done.

Once you have created the best experience possible for your customers, you'll see better results from all of your marketing activities.

Learning Activity:

1. Review all your notes and worksheets from the course, including the maps you've created and other information about what you consider the ideal customer experience for your business.

2. Next, make a list of the actions you will take as soon as you get back to work. Identify the most important tasks that will lead to the biggest potential payoff.

3. Set deadlines for each of the tasks you identified.

CHAPTER 8

Bonus

The Ideal Customer Experience Journey features a step-by-step guide to creating a simple map of your customer's experience with your company. You'll be able to pinpoint the problem spots your customer faces. Armed with that info, you can establish an ideal customer experience that will lay the foundation for a lifetime of business success.

We've divided up the course into simple, bite-size sections so you'll be able to master the content with ease!

The Ideal Customer Experience Journey also offers the following *FREE BONUSES*:

- BONUS #1: *A Workbook* to take notes and complete the activities, along with a *Summary Checklist* to keep track of your progress.

- BONUS #2: *FREE REPORT*, 14 Places Where Your Content Impacts Your Customer's Experience."

- BONUS #3: *Customer Experience Infographic*-- Ready-made outline breaking down the lessons for easy learning.

- BONUS #4: *FREE RESOURCES GUIDE*, Customer Experience Mapping Tools--comprehensive guide on what's available to help you map customer experience.

To receive your FREE bonuses, join our email list at –
amazon@ebusinessmarketinggroup.com

We believe you'll find *The Ideal Customer Experience Journey* an invaluable tool for transforming your customer relations.

We'd love to hear your honest feedback on our product. Leave a review on Amazon, and tell us what you think!

ABOUT THE AUTHOR

Alberto Rocha is on a mission to empower small and midsize businesses throughout the world to master the minutiae of marketing success.

Based in San Francisco, he's known for taking the long view with his clients. Carefully attending and listening to the client's current situation, he tailors his services so that the client can achieve all of his or her goals, from short-term to long-term.

Now he's expanded his problem-solving approach to a new guide, *The Ideal Customer Experience Journey*, so that everyone can benefit from some of the solutions he's delivered. Feel free to shoot Alberto a message, at *ceo@ebusinessmarketinggroup.com*.

www.ingramcontent.com/pod-product-compliance
Lightning Source LLC
Chambersburg PA
CBHW040843180526
45159CB00001B/299